between friends

Andrews McMeel
Publishing

Kansas City

For information, write
Andrews McMeel Publishing,
an Andrews McMeel Universal company,
4520 Main Street, Kansas City, Missouri 64111.

ISBN: 0-7407-2283-2

Library of Congress Catalog Card Number:
2001096505

Produced by Smallwood & Stewart, Inc.
New York City

Written and Compiled by Deborah Schupack
Designed by Carol Bokuniewicz

Of all possessions *a friend*
is the most precious.

Herodotus

A friend may well be reckoned
the masterpiece of Nature.

Ralph Waldo Emerson

You can date the evolving
life of a mind, like the age
of a tree, by the rings of
friendship formed by the
expanding central trunk.

Mary McCarthy

Friendship,
"the wine of life," should,
like a well-stocked cellar, be
continually renewed.

James Boswell

Friendship

in every mar

and remembe

lightning in p

s evanescent

s experience,

red like heat

ast summers.

Henry David Thoreau

Friendship is one of the
most tangible things in a
world which offers fewer
and fewer supports.

Kenneth Branagh

Friends are the DNA of society. They are the basic building blocks of life.

Jerry Seinfeld

Friendship is a
common belief in the same
fallacies, mountebanks,
and hobgoblins.

H. L. Mencken

Love is blind;
friendship closes its eyes.

Anonymous

To be friends with camel owners, you cannot live in huts with low doors.

Punjabi proverb

Love is only chatter,
Friends are all that matter.

Gelett Burgess

Friendship

cement tha

hold the wo

is the only

t will ever

rld together.

Woodrow Wilson

A true friend
is never a burden.

None is so rich as to throw away *a friend*.

Turkish proverb

Love is like the wild rose-briar; *friendship* like the holly-tree. The holly is dark when the rose-briar blooms, but which will bloom most constantly?

Emily Brontë

Good friendships are fragile things that require as much care as any other fragile and precious thing.

Randolph Bourne

Extraordinary creature!
So close *a friend,*
and yet so remote.

Thomas Mann

The best

make frier

you nee

ime to

ds is before

d them.

Ethel Barrymore

The real test of friendship is:
Can you literally do nothing
with the other person?
Can you enjoy together
those moments of life that
are utterly simple? They
are the moments people look
back on at the end of life
and number as their most
sacred experiences.

Eugene Kennedy

The better part of one's life
consists of *friendships*.

Abraham Lincoln

It is not so much our
friends' help that helps us
as the confident knowledge
that they will help us.

Epicurus

Don't walk in front of me;
I may not follow. Don't
walk behind me; I may not
lead. Walk beside me
and just be *my friend*.

Albert Camus

Give an

make goo

d take

d friends.

Epicurus

Be courteous to all,
but intimate with few, and
let those few be well tried
before you give them your
confidence. *True friendship*
is a plant of slow growth,
and must undergo and
withstand the shocks
of adversity before it is
entitled to the appellation.

George Washington

Friends have a way

eaking without words.

Alice Dalgliesh

With a *true friend* everything becomes an adventure.

Aries

March 21 – April 19

Friendship profile: In any circle of friends, the grand plans usually come from you. You do love adventure! But remember, sometimes your friends need a sympathetic ear—rather than invitations to go out and party.

Friendship profile: You are the zodiac's dependable friend. Your friends all know they can turn to you when they're in need—unless what they need is encouragement to take a risk. You are one risk-averse bull!

Taurus

April 20 – May 20

Friendship profile: Ah, the life of the party. With so many interests, you connect with anyone and everyone. All those connections, though, sometimes make you a scatterbrained friend—not the one to leave the keys with at a party.

Gemini

May 21-June 21

Friendship profile: Touchy, touchy. You are one thin-skinned (or shall we say, thin-shelled) crab. But your sensitivity can also be a plus—you are sympathetic and bend over backward (sideways?) not to hurt feelings.

June 22 - July 22

Cancer

Leo

July 23–August 22

Friendship profile: Lead and your friends shall follow. That's because they love your confidence, ambition, and commanding presence. What they don't love, however, is when you become overbearing or arrogant. Ego in moderation, please!

Friendship profile:

You're highly organized—a perfectionist, really—in all aspects of your life, and your friendships are no different. You're the friend who's always cleaning up after a party. (Maybe even after your hosts have gone to bed!)

Virgo

August 23 - September 22

Libra

September 23 - October 22

Friendship profile: You bring a certain spark—friendly, popular, creative—to any group of friends. But notice how they don't turn to you for decisions? That's because you're indecisive. Or are you compromising? No, definitely indecisive. Or, maybe compromising.

Capricorn

December 22–January 19

Friendship profile: It's nice to have an organized, dependable friend like you—one who not only notices favors, but repays them in kind. But try not to feel burdened by your dependability. That's when you come off as calculating and rigid.

Friendship profile:
You are a true original. In fact, sometimes so original that your friends don't know what to make of you (but they love you anyway). You are always marching to a different drummer, which can mean that sometimes you're marching alone!

Aquarius
January 20 - February 18

Friendship profile: **A mystery wrapped in an enigma. That's what your friends say about you. All those covert operations can make you seem manipulative at times, though plenty of people are drawn to your magnetic intensity.**

Scorpio

October 23 - November 21

Friendship profile: **Fun, fun, fun. You are always game to go paint the town, even when you—ooops!— already had other plans. Your friends know that although they can't always count on you, they can count on you for fun.**

Sagittarius

November 22 - December 21